THE PASSING
OF THE CIVIL RIGHTS ACT OF 1964

by Xina M. Uhl

Content Consultant
William P. Jones
Department of History
University of Wisconsin Madison

Core Library

An Imprint of Abdo Publishing
abdopublishing.com

abdopublishing.com

Published by Abdo Publishing, a division of ABDO, PO Box 398166, Minneapolis, Minnesota 55439. Copyright © 2016 by Abdo Consulting Group, Inc. International copyrights reserved in all countries. No part of this book may be reproduced in any form without written permission from the publisher. Core Library™ is a trademark and logo of Abdo Publishing.

Printed in the United States of America, North Mankato, Minnesota

042015
092015

Cover Photo: AP Images
Interior Photos: AP Images, 1, 7, 18, 31, 37, 45; Bill Hudson/AP Images, 4; North Wind Picture Archives, 12; Red Line Editorial, 15, 23; Bettmann/Corbis, 20, 22, 39, 40, 43; Henry Griffin/AP Images, 25; Bill Allen/AP Images, 28; Everett Collection/Newscom, 32; Horace Cort/AP Images, 34

Editor: Mirella Miller
Series Designer: Becky Daum

Library of Congress Control Number: 2015931188

Cataloging-in-Publication Data
Uhl, Xina M.
 The passing of the Civil Rights Act of 1964 / Xina M. Uhl.
   p. cm. -- (Stories of the civil rights movement)
Includes bibliographical references and index.
ISBN 978-1-62403-883-9
1. African Americans--Civil rights--History--20th century--Juvenile literature.
2. Segregation--Law and legislation--United States--History--20th century--Juvenile literature. 3. United States. Civil Rights Act of 1964--Juvenile literature. 4. Civil rights--United States--History--Juvenile literature. I. Title.
342.73--dc23
                                                        2015931188

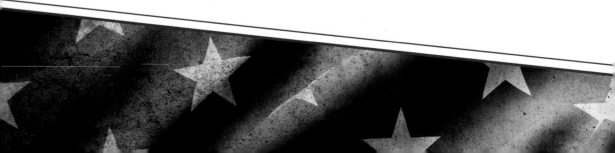

CONTENTS

CHAPTER ONE
The Children's Crusade 4

CHAPTER TWO
The Beginning of Segregation .12

CHAPTER THREE
A Fateful Day 20

CHAPTER FOUR
The Argument Over Civil Rights 28

CHAPTER FIVE
The Aftermath 34

Snapshot of the Civil Rights Act of 1964 .... .42

Stop and Think .... .44

Glossary 46

Learn More .... .47

Index .... .48

About the Author .... .48

THE CHILDREN'S CRUSADE

It was 1963 in Birmingham, Alabama. One by one, African-American children skipped school to show up at the 16th Street Baptist Church. They ranged in age from 12 to 18 years old. The children had decided it was time to take a stand. They were tired of hatred and unfair laws.

Soon the group grew to nearly 1,000 African-American children. Adults were absent.

Police lead a group of African-American children to jail after they protested discrimination in May 1963.

The children's parents feared they would lose their jobs if they protested discrimination. Their children showed up at the church. The group planned to march 0.5 miles (0.8 km) to City Hall. Few made it that far.

The children began a peaceful march. White police officers tried to stop the demonstration. But the children were determined. They continued on. The children wanted an end to segregation. The police arrested hundreds of children and took them to jail in school buses. They beat others with clubs or attacked them with police dogs. The protests went on for more than one week.

The rest of the United States saw these events on the news. The sight of peaceful protesters being attacked outraged many Americans. The adults in charge of organizing the Alabama protest sat down with Birmingham officials and President John F. Kennedy. The city agreed to allow African Americans into downtown stores. They also released the protesters from jail. The protesters agreed to stop

Police officers blasted protesters in Birmingham with high-pressure fire hoses.

marching. Although this was not a complete victory, this event pushed the civil rights movement forward.

Separate Lives

Life during the early 1960s was very different for African Americans and whites. African Americans usually lived in poorer neighborhoods. In many southern states, laws kept African Americans from using the same facilities as whites. Public areas such as grocery stores, churches, movie theaters, schools, and restaurants had separate areas for each race. This was called segregation. Some states also outlawed marriage between different races. If African Americans broke these laws, known as Jim Crow laws, they were beaten or killed. The laws were created to make African Americans feel like second-class citizens.

Civil rights workers and leaders such as Martin Luther King Jr. worked to change these laws. They scored a major Supreme Court victory in 1954 with *Brown v. Board of Education of Topeka*. The case outlawed segregation in schools.

Jim Crow Laws

Jim Crow laws were in place from the 1880s through the 1960s. They required that African Americans and whites use separate schools, public places, transportation, restrooms, and drinking fountains. In some places, African-American hospital patients were even kept separate from whites. African-American public spaces were usually of lower quality than those reserved for whites.

A large problem remained, though. Who would make schools and towns in the South obey the law? Change came slowly. Advocates of civil rights felt the progress was too slow.

A New President

John F. Kennedy became president in 1961. King and others hoped the new president would help their cause. Seventy percent of African Americans voted for him. But President Kennedy worried that acting on civil rights would cause him trouble. Southern lawmakers might not support him. Neither would whites across the country who supported segregation.

CIVIL RIGHTS VOICES
Martin Luther King Jr.

. . . when you have seen hate-filled policemen curse, kick and even kill your black brothers and sisters . . . you can understand our . . . impatience.

The Reverend Martin Luther King Jr. helped lead the civil rights movement in the United States. By using peaceful protests, he drew attention to segregation and discrimination faced by African Americans. His actions helped pass the Civil Rights Act of 1964. In 1968 he was shot and killed in Tennessee.

Civil rights leaders continued to protest. King called Birmingham the most segregated city in the country. Nearly 1,000 people were arrested, including King. President Kennedy sent in the Alabama National Guard to keep the peace.

President Kennedy decided he had to do something about civil rights. In June 1963, he put together a bill that would later become the Civil Rights Act of 1964.

The bill would take segregation apart piece by piece. All Americans would have equal chances to use public places. There would be no more all-white schools. Voting would be protected. The lives of African Americans would change forever if the bill passed. The bill moved to Congress with President Kennedy's support. But then Kennedy was assassinated in November 1963. The fate of the bill became uncertain.

In 1963 President Kennedy began working on a bill that would end segregation across the United States. He gave these remarks about the proposed law:

> The heart of the question is . . . whether we are going to treat our fellow Americans as we want to be treated. If an American, because his skin is dark, cannot eat lunch in a restaurant open to the public, if he cannot send his children to the best public school available, if he cannot vote for the public officials who will represent him, if, in short, he cannot enjoy the full and free life which all of us want, then who among us would be content to have the color of his skin changed and stand in his place? . . .
>
> One hundred years of delay have passed since President Lincoln freed the slaves, yet their heirs, their grandsons, are not fully free . . . this Nation, for all its hopes and all its boasts, will not be fully free until all its citizens are free.

Source: "Report to the American People on Civil Rights, 11 June 1963." John F. Kennedy Presidential Library and Museum. *John F. Kennedy Presidential Library and Museum, June 11, 1963. Web. Accessed February 17, 2015.*

Changing Minds

Imagine you support President Kennedy's upcoming bill. How would you defend his ideas to people who disagreed with him? Make sure you explain your opinion. Include facts and details that support your reasons.

CHAPTER TWO

THE BEGINNING OF SEGREGATION

In the early 1600s, ships brought the first African slaves to the North American colonies established by Great Britain. Most slaves arrived between 1720 and 1780. In 1776, the colonists formed the United States of America. Many white citizens of the new nation argued that African Americans were less human. Whites forced the Africans into slavery and made them work hard labor for no pay.

Many slaves in the South were forced to pick cotton or other crops.

Most slaves lived in the Southern states and worked on farms. Over time, Northern states outlawed slavery. It remained legal in the Southern states. This split led to the American Civil War (1861–1865). The North won the war and passed a law banning slavery across the nation. Although the slaves were now free, they still had a long fight for equality ahead of them.

Soon after the American Civil War, amendments to the US Constitution were passed to try to fix problems for African Americans. The Fourteenth and Fifteenth Amendments made African Americans citizens and protected their right to vote. Despite these amendments, however, segregation became commonplace. *Plessy v. Ferguson*, a Supreme Court case decided in 1895, made segregation legal.

African Americans continued to work toward equality. After World War II (1939–1945), change began happening. African Americans resisted segregation through peaceful protests. They and their

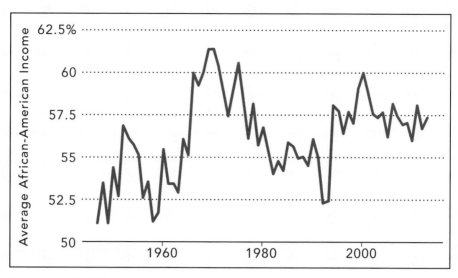

Income Differences

This chart shows the average African-American income as a percentage of the average white income. How has African-American income changed over the years? What events happened during these years? Do you think they had an effect on the change you see here?

supporters called on Congress every year from 1945 to 1957 to pass a civil rights bill. The Civil Rights Act of 1957 was passed, followed by the Civil Rights Act of 1960. These bills were aimed at fixing problems that kept African Americans from voting. They were not strong enough to fix the issue of segregation, though.

Protests Continue

African Americans worked hard for change. In 1955 an African-American woman named Rosa Parks was arrested in Montgomery, Alabama. She refused to give up her bus seat to a white person. In order to stop such segregation, African Americans refused to ride city buses. African Americans wanted Montgomery and the bus companies to get rid of the bus segregation laws. The case went to the Supreme Court. In 1956, the Supreme Court ruled that segregation on public buses violated the Constitution of the United States. This ruling gave civil rights leaders hope to move forward with other protests.

Opposition

Russell Long, a Louisiana senator, revealed his objection to ending segregation during a debate on the Senate floor. He spoke about how some whites believed it was okay to marry blacks, but others did not. What if these whites were pressured to marry someone from another race? He feared people would be pressured to marry people from another race if legal segregation ended.

These peaceful protests included sit-ins. In 1960 four black college students in North Carolina made the news. They sat down at a white lunch counter and refused to leave. The next day, 24 students sat at the same counter. Sit-ins were soon happening in seven states across the country.

Many changes could not happen if African Americans were not able to vote. The ability to vote keeps the government working for all of its people. But threats of violence had kept many African Americans in the South from voting. Civil rights groups worked to register them to vote. It was a dangerous job. Beatings, deaths, and arrests could—and did—happen.

Peaceful Protests

Martin Luther King Jr. believed in peaceful protests. He first learned about the idea of nonviolence in school. There he read the work of Henry David Thoreau, an American author who wrote in the mid 1800s. Thoreau wrote about refusing to go along with an evil system. King believed that racism and segregation were evil.

Thousands of people gathered in Washington, DC, to show support for the civil rights movement in August 1963.

In August 1963, approximately 250,000 people gathered in Washington, DC, for the March on Washington for Jobs and Freedom. Civil rights leaders urged lawmakers to pass President Kennedy's civil rights bill and to strengthen it by prohibiting discrimination in employment. They spoke about being turned away from jobs because of their skin color. The civil rights movement was gathering speed. The next stop was Congress.

During the March on Washington, Martin Luther King Jr. gave a speech to the crowd. His "I Have a Dream" speech became famous for its power and passion. In it, King quoted song lyrics from the spiritual "Free at Last":

Free at last, free at last
I thank God I'm free at last
Free at last, free at last
I thank God I'm free at last
Way down yonder in the graveyard walk
I thank God I'm free at last
Me and my Jesus going to meet and talk
I thank God I'm free at last
Some of these mornings, bright and fair
I thank God I'm free at last
Gon' meet King Jesus in the air
I thank God I'm free at last

Source: J. W. Work. "Free at Last." Negrospirituals.com. Spiritual Workshop, n.d. Web. Accessed February 17, 2015.

What's the Big Idea?

Take a close look at these lyrics. What is the main idea of this song? Why do you think Martin Luther King Jr. included these lyrics in his famous speech? What message does the song give?

CHAPTER THREE

A FATEFUL DAY

Nothing seemed out of the ordinary on November 22, 1963. President John F. Kennedy and his wife, Jackie, were visiting Dallas, Texas, to talk about the issues they supported. They drove through the city waving at the crowd as they rode in a convertible. Suddenly shots rang out. Kennedy and Texas Governor John Connally, seated next to him, were struck with bullets from a rifle. Kennedy

President Kennedy rides through Dallas moments before he is killed.

President Kennedy needed support from both political parties to pass the civil rights bill.

was rushed to the hospital, but it was too late. At 1:00 p.m., he was declared dead. Still wearing her bloodstained pink suit, Jackie Kennedy stood beside Vice President Lyndon B. Johnson as he took the oath to become the nation's 36th president. Supporters of the civil rights bill were worried. Johnson was a southerner. His track record on civil rights seemed uncertain. What would the future hold?

Writing of the Bill

Months earlier, President Kennedy had drafted the bill that would later become the Civil Rights Act of 1964. Congress needed to solve the serious problem of

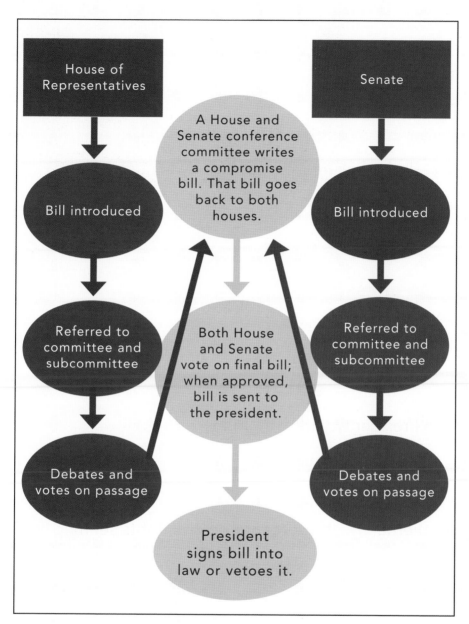

How a Bill Becomes a Law

Several thousand bills are introduced to Congress every year. Only approximately 150 of them become law. Above you will find a diagram that shows the path a bill goes through. At each step, a bill may fail, which is why so few become laws.

discrimination. It also needed to keep politics in mind. Both Democratic and Republican votes were needed for the bill to pass.

Soon after President Kennedy announced the bill, 42 senators pledged to support it. Next it went to committees in the House of Representatives and the Senate. Both committees changed the bill. Now it contained 11 different titles, or sections. The titles would give power to the courts to stop job discrimination. Segregation would also be illegal in public places and programs. The titles also stated that committees would be set up to put an end to these problems.

The Difference Between an Act and a Law

Both houses of Congress pass an act. It becomes law when the president approves it, or because it is passed over his veto. The term "act" is also used for a bill that has been passed by just one House of Congress. A law is a rule of conduct that can be set up by a community, state, or nation. Different kinds of officials make sure that laws are obeyed. Some examples are city police officers, county sheriffs, or federal marshals.

Representative Howard W. Smith attempted to slow movement of the civil rights bill by making changes to it.

The Bill Moves Ahead

Less than one week after becoming president, President Johnson spoke to Congress. The best way to honor Kennedy, he said, would be to pass his civil rights bill. Johnson's support helped the bill, and it moved to the House floor for debate in just two weeks. A change took place there. Howard W. Smith, a southern Democratic representative, added gender to a section of the bill. This section, Title VII, would stop gender discrimination during job hiring. The bill passed, 289 to 126 votes. This was a big win, but the bill still needed to pass through the Senate before it became official.

Roadblocks in the Senate

The bill faced a big roadblock in the Senate. Opponents started a filibuster. A filibuster is an attempt to block Senate action by making several speeches about a bill. In 1964 southern Democratic senators took over the Senate floor and talked nonstop. They would keep talking until

---

Famous Filibusters of the Past

Senator Huey Long was a Democrat from Louisiana. In 1935 he spoke for more than 15 hours straight during a filibuster. He read recipes for cornbread and turnip greens. Glen Taylor was a Democrat from Idaho. In 1947 he talked for more than eight hours about his children, fishing, baptism, and Wall Street. Senator Strom Thurmond holds the longest record for filibustering. This Democratic senator from South Carolina spoke for 24 hours and 18 minutes. He was protesting the Civil Rights Act of 1957.

the bill was dropped or changed in a way they agreed with. The debate could be ended only if a two-thirds majority voted to end it. Such a vote is known as cloture. Filibusters are rare, and cloture was even rarer. Cloture had never been used before for a civil rights bill.

EXPLORE ONLINE

Chapter Three focuses on the content of the Civil Rights Act of 1964. The main parts of the bill were split into titles. As you know, every source is different. Check out the website below to see what it says about the bill's titles. How is the information on the website presented differently from the information in the chapter? How is it the same? What new information did you learn from the website?

Civil Rights Act of 1964
mycorelibrary.com/civil-rights-act

CHAPTER FOUR

THE ARGUMENT OVER CIVIL RIGHTS

As with many bills, Kennedy's civil rights bill faced sharp political opposition. Both sides made sure their arguments were heard in Congress. As the filibuster went on, the bill continued to be discussed in homes, schools, and across the country.

Arguments against the Bill

Those opposed to the bill had many fears. They worried about the increase in the federal

Arguments for both sides of the bill, including by Republican senator John Sherman Cooper, were presented to Congress before the bill was eventually passed.

government's power. This would reduce the power of the states. Other people thought people of different races would be forced to marry. Then there were those who said people would not obey the law no matter what was passed.

Business owners did not like the idea of new laws. They wanted to do things their own way. Some said they already hired African Americans. They felt the bill was not needed.

Underlying much of the opposition were deep feelings of racism. For centuries, people had discriminated against African Americans. Many

Roy Wilkins

In 1963 Roy Wilkins was the Executive Director of the National Association for the Advancement of Colored People. On July 22, he stood before a Senate committee to explain life under segregation. He used a family road trip as an example. On their trips, white families did not worry that they would not be served at hotels and stores. The same was not true for African Americans. Some hotels would not serve them. They could not use restrooms at some places or buy treats at every shop.

Rallies across the country were held in support of the civil rights bill.

of these people resisted changes that would put African Americans on an equal footing with whites.

Arguments for the Bill

The nation watched as the filibuster wore on. Civil rights leaders such as Martin Luther King Jr. stood strong in the bill's support. A huge rally took place at Georgetown University. Jewish and Christian leaders both took part in it. The bill was a subject at many church services.

Dirksen gave a heartfelt speech to the Senate to help the Civil Rights Act pass.

Some Republicans and some Democrats supported the bill, while other members of the parties opposed it. President Johnson worked to change their minds. The bill's supporters made several changes to the bill while the filibuster went on. Most of these reduced penalties for those who did not follow the law. Instead they rewarded those who followed the law. It seemed like a good compromise.

The Final Vote

The leader of the Republican Party, Illinois Senator Everett Dirksen, took this updated bill to the Senate. If he could change some minds, the bill would pass. Cloture needed 67 votes. Every member of the Senate showed up to vote. It passed with 71 votes. The 57-day filibuster was over. Next, the civil rights bill went to President Johnson to sign. On July 2, 1964, the Civil Rights Act of 1964 became law.

CIVIL RIGHTS VOICES
Everett Dirksen

There was a South of slavery and secession—that South is dead. There is a South of union and freedom—that South, thank God, is living, breathing, growing every hour.

Everett Dirksen began his time in Congress in the House of Representatives. After several terms, he was elected to the Senate. In 1959 he became the Republican minority leader. During the debate over the Civil Rights Act of 1964, he urged an end to the filibuster. He served in Congress until his death in 1969.

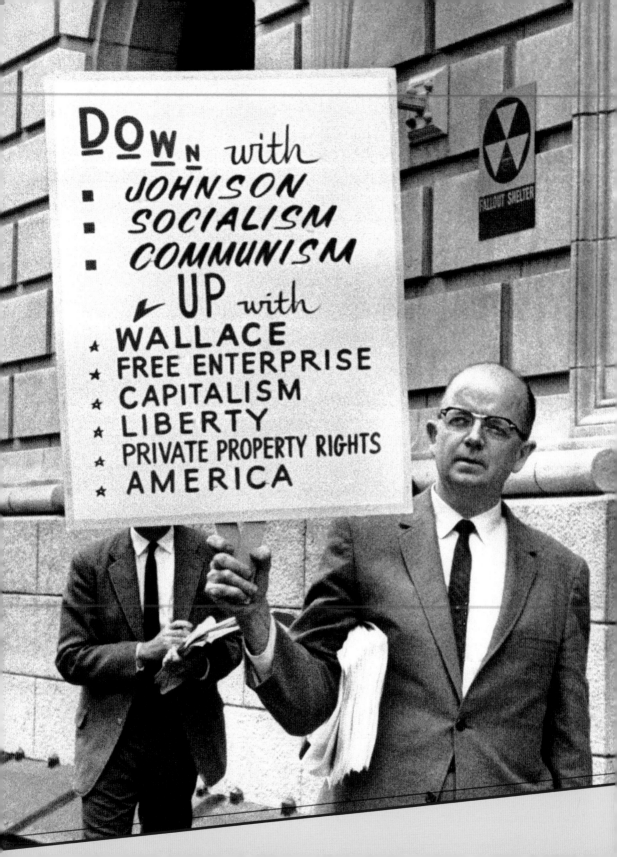

CHAPTER FIVE

THE AFTERMATH

Lester Maddox lived in Atlanta, Georgia. He ran a café there called the Pickrick Cafeteria. He believed strongly in segregation. Now that it was against the law, he grew angry. In 1964 three African-American college students tested the law. They tried to enter the Pickrick Cafeteria. Maddox chased them out with a gun. His white customers chased the African-American students with axe

To avoid having to serve African Americans, Lester Maddox chose to close his restaurant.

handles. Maddox was not the only person unhappy with the passing of the Civil Rights Act of 1964. Many white southerners were upset. Maddox was charged with assault. The jury at his trial was all white. They found him not guilty. He went on to become governor of Georgia.

Allan Bakke

When Allan Bakke, a white man, applied to study at a California medical school, he was rejected twice. He sued in 1978, saying that the school had discriminated against him with its affirmative action policies. He said that he had suffered from discrimination. The Supreme Court ruled that affirmative action was constitutional, as long as it did not set specific quotas, such as for race. Bakke entered the school. Later, he became a doctor.

Effects of the Act

The passing of the Civil Rights Act of 1964 was a victory for civil rights. Change happened almost overnight. Doors opened to African Americans. Segregation stopped in public places, and discrimination on the job became illegal. Incomes for African Americans grew. This was also true for Native Americans,

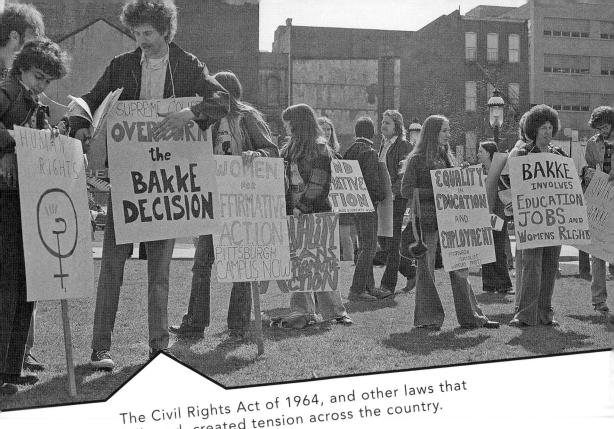

The Civil Rights Act of 1964, and other laws that followed, created tension across the country.

Asians, and Latinos. Women's rights also made great strides.

Congress could now deny funding to states that refused to follow the law. They used this same idea in future bills. The Equal Employment Opportunity Commission was set up. It stops on-the-job discrimination. The act also laid the basis for affirmative action. This policy makes jobs more accessible to minorities and women. Colleges also apply affirmative action policies to admit more minorities. Early on, these policies created some issues, as was the case with Allan Bakke. Affirmative action is not a law. Instead, it is a group of policies and programs that apply to businesses that receive money from the federal government. Because of this, the businesses have to follow federal rules on discrimination.

Future Work

The Civil Rights Act of 1964 did not fix all civil rights issues overnight. It did not offer enough protection for African Americans who still faced danger for voting. The Voting Rights Act of 1965 solved many of these

The passing of civil rights laws in the 1960s cleared the way for increased voting participation by African Americans.

The Civil Rights Act of 1964 helped the civil rights movement significantly, but many changes are still happening today.

problems. The number of African-American voters increased greatly afterward.

The process of protest and debate that brought about the Civil Rights Act of 1964 is still alive and well. Its influence will continue in the future.

FURTHER EVIDENCE

Chapter Five covers what happened after the Civil Rights Act of 1964 was passed. Identify the main points of this chapter. What key evidence supports these points? The website at the link below talks about affirmative action, one of the subjects covered here. Learn more about different points of view on this subject. What does the text say about it? What other details have you learned by reading this page?

Affirmative Action

mycorelibrary.com/civil-rights-act

Lawmakers and supporters stand around President Johnson in the White House. As they look on, the president signs the bill into law.

Date

July 2, 1964

Key Players

President John F. Kennedy, President Lyndon B. Johnson, members of Congress, Martin Luther King Jr.

What Happened

President Kennedy had proposed a civil rights bill that would stop segregation of African Americans and whites. The next president, Lyndon B. Johnson, supported the bill. Following a long series of debates in Congress, the bill was signed into law in 1964.

Impact

The act was a major step forward for the civil rights movement. It outlawed discrimination based on race, color, religion, sex, or national origin. The act banned segregation in public places such as schools. It also changed workplaces by banning discrimination in hiring.

Why Do I Care?

Civil rights struggles did not end in 1964. They are still happening in the United States and in other countries. Ask your parent or guardian about recent civil rights stories in the news. Then learn more about two of those stories by looking them up online, in a newspaper, or by visiting your local library. How are civil rights struggles different now?

Take a Stand

This book includes information about people who stood up for what they believed in. Look through the book and locate where the following people took a stand, and why: Martin Luther King Jr., Lyndon B. Johnson, Rosa Parks, and Lester Maddox. Write a sentence about each person's stand. Do you agree with what they did? Why or why not?

Say What?

Studying the Civil Rights Act of 1964 can mean learning a lot of new vocabulary. Find five words in this book you've never heard before. Use a dictionary to find out what they mean. Then write the meanings in your own words, and use each word in a new sentence.

You Are There

This book discusses the Children's Crusade. Imagine that you are a boy or girl living in Birmingham, Alabama, during this march. Write a letter to your friends telling them what you saw. Be sure to add plenty of detail to your notes.

GLOSSARY

amendments
changes or additions to a document, such as the US Constitution

assassination
the murder of an important person

cloture
a vote to end a filibuster

discrimination
denying people the right to do something or be somewhere because of their race, age, or other factors

filibuster
to use delays to put off or prevent lawmaking

minority leader
the leader of the political party that has fewer members in the US Senate or House of Representatives

racism
a belief that race defines certain values and traits of people, and that one race is more important than another

segregation
the practice of keeping different races apart from each other

sit-ins
protests where people sit in a place until they are given what they want

LEARN MORE

Books

Bader, Bonnie. *Who Was Martin Luther King, Jr.?* New York: Grosset & Dunlap, 2008.

Turck, Mary. *The Civil Rights Movement for Kids: A History with 21 Activities.* Chicago: Chicago Review Press, 2000.

Wiles, Deborah. *Freedom Summer: Celebrating the 50th Anniversary of the Freedom Summer.* New York: Atheneum Books for Young Readers, 2014.

Websites

To learn more about Stories of the Civil Rights Movement, visit **booklinks.abdopublishing.com**. These links are routinely monitored and updated to provide the most current information available.

Visit **mycorelibrary.com** for free additional tools for teachers and students.

INDEX

affirmative action, 36, 37–38, 41

Bakke, Allan, 36, 38
Birmingham, Alabama, 5–6, 10
Brown v. Board of Education of Topeka, 8–9

Children's Crusade, 5–7
Civil Rights Act of 1957, 15, 26
Civil Rights Act of 1960, 15
cloture, 27, 33
Congress, 10, 15, 18, 22, 23, 24, 25, 29, 33, 37
Constitution, US, 14, 16

Dirksen, Everett, 33
discrimination, 6, 9, 18, 24, 26, 30, 36–38

Equal Employment Opportunity Commission, 37

filibusters, 26–27, 29, 31–32, 33

gender, 25–26

Johnson, Lyndon B., 22, 25, 32, 33, 38

Kennedy, John F., 6, 9–10, 11, 18, 21–22, 24, 25, 29, 38
King, Martin Luther, Jr., 8–10, 17, 19, 31

Long, Russell, 16

Maddox, Lester, 35–36

peaceful protests, 6, 9, 14, 17

schools, 5, 8–10, 11, 29, 36
segregation, 6, 8–10, 11, 14–15, 16, 17, 24, 30, 35, 36
slaves, 11, 13–14, 33
Smith, Howard W., 25
Supreme Court, 8, 14, 16, 36

Voting Rights Act of 1965, 38

Wilkins, Roy, 30

ABOUT THE AUTHOR

Xina Uhl loves history, hiking, travel, and pizza. She lives in southern California with her husband and a bunch of dogs.